The Starting Five

Five Essentials to Make
the Team Better

John Blankenship

Dwaine Cales

Avid Readers Publishing Group

Lakewood, California

The Starting Five

Avid Readers Publishing Group

http://www.avidreaderspg.com

ISBN-13: 978-1-61286-367-2

Printed in the United States

Introduction

The Starting Five is a book for athletes that desire to learn how to lead their teams effectively. It is also a resource for coaches to use to help their captains understand leadership in a way that will move their team in a positive direction. Combining over 30 years of coaching experience, Dr. Cales and I have evaluated some of the best players that have led our teams. After carefully analyzing those leaders, we have determined the five most important qualities a captain must possess.

This book will be centered around explaining those five leadership qualities in an easy to understand format. That very format is what makes this book unique from other books. We have written the main part in story form with the hope that this will make it both easier to understand and more engaging. We believe you will find the book enjoyable to read but, more importantly, effective in helping you better understand how to lead your team and what is expected of you as a captain.

It is great to be selected as captains for your team. That usually means one of two things. First, you are a senior, and as a result of simply showing up for four years, you have been given the position of a captain. Second, the coach or team has seen leadership potential in you and has chosen you to be a captain. Either way, you are in the position of leading the team. Congratulations! Now what do you? How do you lead? Where do you start? Our research has led us to believe most players are neither taught how to lead nor what it means to be a captain. Some of the questions that might surface are: What are your new responsibilities? How do you get your teammates on board? How do you approach the coach with issues or concerns? How do you raise the work ethic and performance expectations? How do you begin changing the culture of the team? These are some of the topics that will be covered throughout the book.

The development of these five leadership traits will certainly make you and your team better, and that's great news. The better news is, these traits can carry over to all aspects of your life. Learning and developing them now will make you a better spouse, parent, and employee in the future. Good luck leading your teams!

Chapter 1 – The Game Plan

"Hey Alex, can you believe the season is about to start in a few days?"

"I know, right. I can't believe it myself. I certainly hope this year goes a whole lot better than last season. Losing several games was bad enough, but the team captains we had made the season even less enjoyable. Dylan, we are supposed to meet with coach in 15 minutes. If he doesn't talk to us about this year's leadership, should we bring it up to him?"

"Alex, I don't think we have any choice. I do NOT want a repeat from last year. That was absolutely miserable. I know this is Coach Jones' first year, but I really like what he talked about to the team during the offseason. I think he will be open to our input about positive leadership from the team. Let's go to the meeting and see what he has to say."

"Hi Coach Jones, we are here for the meeting you requested."

"Hi Dylan and Alex, thank you both for coming. You are even a few minutes early. I really appreciate that as it shows respect for my time. I will also respect your time and will get right to the point. We are going to be selecting captains soon. I'm going to be presenting some material for consideration for those who might be selected. Could you two join us for that?"

"Sure we can, coach. We are definitely interested. We're anxious to hear your thoughts about what is expected of the captains. In past years it meant the captains would lead the team on the court, and they would also meet with the refs before the game, but that was about it."

"I appreciate your interest and desire to be team leaders. With this being my first year coaching this team, I want to make sure our captains are prepared to lead. You can rest assured their responsibilities will be much greater than leading the team on the court and talking to the refs.

"I enjoyed coaching this team during the summer. It was beneficial for me to get a feel for the capabilities of the individual players, as well as team chemistry and leadership potential. Dylan and Alex, I have no doubt you two are the people I want leading this team for the next couple of years. After coaching for more than 20 years, I have determined the five most critical leadership traits captains need to develop if they want to successfully lead their teams. I want to begin explaining and teaching those to both of you. It will take time and commitment on your part. If you guys are willing to do that, we can start building a great team culture around here."

"Coach, Alex and I were just talking about that very thing before coming to see you. This past summer we mentioned to you about how our captains from last year created drama, they weren't encouraging, and certainly did not lead by example. We don't want to duplicate that style of leadership."

"I planned to meet with more than just you two, but I am even more confident that I want you two leading this team. Are you both willing to accept the position of captains? If so, we will begin the process. I will announce you guys as team captains at our first practice next week.

We'll have our first meeting Saturday morning at 9:00 in the gym. Plan on being here most of the day as it will take several hours to discuss the five points of leadership. I will have one of my assistant coaches pick up some pizza for lunch. Let's work hard together and

4

make sure your teammates have positive things to say about you two after this season. Enjoy the rest of your week, and I will see you Saturday morning."

"Thanks, Coach Jones. We will be here. See you then."

"Hey Dylan, can you pick me up Saturday morning so we can talk before we meet with coach?"

"Yes, I will swing by your house around 8:30 Saturday morning."

"Sounds good, I will call you later so we can talk some more about our meeting and the upcoming season."

Both Alex and Dylan could not stop thinking about Saturday's meeting. For the first time in a while they were excited about basketball starting. They always enjoyed playing, but Coach Jones had given them reason to believe things would be different this year.

"Good morning, Alex."

"Good morning, Dylan. Thanks for picking me up today. I thought it would be wise to touch base before heading in for our meeting with Coach."

"Good idea, Alex. I have been thinking about the meeting all week. I already feel like this year is going to be different, in a good way."

"Me too, and I am really excited."

Alex and Dylan arrived at school and made their way to the gym. They were early, but Coach Jones was already sitting in the bleachers awaiting their arrival. Dylan and Alex peeked in and saw coach reading through some notes.

"Good morning, Coach."

"Good morning guys. How was your week?"

"It went by fast. We are both excited to get the season started next week. We are also looking forward to learning more about team leadership from these meetings."

"I am also very excited to start the season. I'm really looking forward to practice starting on Monday and visiting with the rest of the team. Let's jump right into things this morning. You guys know from discussions we had this past summer that I have coached at three different schools prior to coming here. I always ask the same question of my players the very first day at a new school. I will ask you two that same question. What kind of training or interaction did you have with your coach in preparation for being captain? The answers I received have been rather interesting. Every person pretty much responded the same. They said they really hadn't thought about it very much, but couldn't say that they had ever received any information or formal training. Most of the athletes said they were always kind of a leader, and it pretty much just happened because they displayed leadership qualities at some level.

"So let's think about this for a moment. Have either of you received training on dribbling? How about shooting? How about passing and defense? So does that cover all the aspects of making our team the best it can be? Go ahead Alex, you don't have to raise your hand."

"Well, Coach, that covers most of the fundamentals of basketball, but I'm not hearing anything about leadership."

"That's a very good observation. Most teams focus only on the offensive and defensive strategies. I want both of you to see the team through the lens of what make us better. Teaching leadership skills will be a core part of what we focus on this year. I'm convinced when the leadership principles I want to teach you are coupled with the basketball fundamentals, it will be a powerful combination."

"Sounds good coach, but where do we begin in this process?"

"Great question, Dylan. I assume you both still desire to serve as captains this year? Did you notice I used the word serve? Part of being a captain is being a servant. We want to approach serving as captain as another aspect of team building that will make our team better."

Alex and Dylan both looked at each other. They knew what the other one was thinking because they both realized this was a different mentality than what the captains had in the past. Coach Jones certainly had their attention at this point.

"Okay Coach. We are listening. If it can make our team better, we are definitely ready to hear what you are thinking."

"Good, let's get into our discussion then. Let me give you an overview of *The Starting Five*: the five aspects of being a captain. We want to build a relationship between the captains and the coach as well as between the captains and the team that sets a higher level of performance. That should also improve our communication, better define the role of the captains, and help determine how the captains should interact with the coach and the team. We need to approach these principles in a way that the team understands and that will create a strong environment of leadership, teamwork, and mutual respect. These are qualities that will make the team better but will also serve you well after you graduate. Does that make sense? What do you think, Dylan?"

"Yeah, coach. That kind of makes sense, but it is certainly different, and I guess we aren't sure just how that happens."

"Okay, that's all I ask. Be willing to listen and keep an open mind. Analyze what you hear from the perspective of DOES THIS MAKE OUR TEAM BETTER? We will start with an overview of the Starting Five, and I would appreciate your input as we work together to develop our team leadership."

"Hey, coach, can I say something first."

"Sure, Alex, what's on your mind?"

"Well, coach, I don't want to put a damper on this. I mean, if it makes our team better, fine. But, I have some reservations about this captain thing. I certainly want to serve as captain, but it seems like more often than not, the people who weren't chosen are ticked, and whoever does get selected starts thinking too highly of themselves, which makes it worse. At least, that's how it's been historically. It never seemed to make the team better in the past. How do we overcome that?"

"Alex, that is the perfect set up for our time together on this part of our team development. Thank you."

"I'm sorry, coach. Are you teasing me? What do you mean?"

"Alex, Brene Brown wrote a great book called *Daring Greatly*. She said, 'vulnerability is a catalyst for courage, compassion and connection.' By saying you

11

questioned being a captain, you were making yourself vulnerable. In making yourself vulnerable, you displayed the courage to question something that possibly others were thinking, but they were afraid to say. Alex, you just showed courage. If we as a team can communicate this year with courage, compassion, and connection, do you think that would make our team better? Do you think that would make the role of captain more valuable to the team?"

"I'm not totally sure what you just said, but I think so."

"Good, let's start thinking about The Starting Five.

"We will definitely list the most important first, and that, of course, is INTEGRITY. If you want to be a leader, it will have to start here. You can do the other four, but without integrity, everything else is hollow. Hypocrisy has no place in leadership. Integrity is the quality of being honest and having strong moral principles. It is honesty. It is honor. It is truthfulness and trustworthiness. Integrity produces unity within the team.

"Did you notice that vulnerability produces connection, and integrity produces unity? Do you think connection and unity makes the team better?"

"Slow down, coach. Let me think about that for a second. What does that look like in a captain?"

"Thanks, Alex. I knew I could count on you. And just briefly, here's what I mean. The captain has to be honest, truthful, and trustworthy in communications with the coach and the team in everything they say and do. They can't say one thing in a meeting with the coach and another with their friends. They can't agree about the way things will be done with the coach but undermine that in practice. When they work on drills, they do them the same when the coach is right there as they do when he isn't. If the team sees this behavior in their captain, it builds unity as everyone communicates and works with the same integrity. Does that make sense?"

"It's starting to Coach. Thanks."

"Great, then let's move on to the second of the Starting Five: Coachability. As you can see, integrity overlaps with coachability. Part of integrity is honor, and honor and coachability go hand in hand. You might think that the second of The Starting Five would be work ethic/skill development, and while that is a very important part of being a captain, the truth is you can't work hard at something if you don't know how to do it. Being coachable helps to build connection and unity with both your teammates and coach. Can you see how coachability builds on integrity? Alex, do you want to make yourself vulnerable again by asking questions?"

"Oh, sure, why not? Ok, let me just play devil's advocate here. What if I don't agree with something you're coaching? I mean, what do I do with that if I'm the captain?"

"Great question, Alex. And yes, that is a real possibility. I mean, we all know I'm perfect, right? That will probably never happen, but let's just say on the off chance that it does, how would you handle that?"

"Hmmmm. I would probably meet with some of my best friends later and complain together and undermine your coaching. I'm just kidding, coach. I don't know, maybe just keep my mouth shut and hope for the best."

"Thanks, Alex. You make a great devil's advocate. But, let's face it, neither of those responses make the team better. What's a third option?"

" Uh… come to you and ask questions and maybe come to a better understanding…. Or maybe you could come to a better understanding of my viewpoint. Well, it was worth a shot to slip that second part in there, coach."

"Okay, Alex, that sounds better. Keep in mind you're in the role of captain, and in that role communication between you and the coach is one of the most important aspects of increasing the value of the captain for the team. You cannot communicate about questions to the team, if you haven't taken responsibility for understanding the coach's point of view. As the captain you have the right to question, and it is this exchange that the relationship between you and the coach grows.

"Dylan and Alex, I really like this quote from Michael Jordan. He said, 'My best skill was that I was coachable. I was a sponge and aggressive to learn.' And don't forget our foundational question: DOES IT MAKE THE TEAM BETTER?"

"That brings us to the third member of The Starting Five, skill development/work ethic. Are you beginning to see how these five are interrelated and can be a definite factor in making the team better?

"Skill development is a series of small measurable accomplishments along the journey. As a captain, it is important for the team to see your dedication to daily work on the fundamentals. Profound dedication to the boring makes a champion. Teams typically want to jump to results and the goal of 'state champions,' but that is really not a goal at all. Today's goal is to keep your sights on what you are doing today. Crossovers, free throws, defensive deflections, can be broken down and worked on over and over and over. Your teammates will be bored and tired and discouraged, and wondering when the fun stuff starts, and that's when you get to be captain. That's when you get the opportunity to shine as a leader. That's when you need to remember the honor of running out first and talking to the refs before the game starts because in leadership, there are a lot more moments of frustration and exhaustion than there are honor and recognition.

"Being a captain is a wonderful opportunity to learn and grow. Being a captain entails being watched as you work on the daily routine over and over and over.

It entails being watched as you interact with your coach. It involves setting a standard that serves as a continual example of hard work, repetition and honor.

"Skill development does not happen without work ethic. You will notice that as we have talked about The Starting Five and the qualities of leadership, we have not mentioned the word talent. Talent in the absence of these five qualities does not create leadership.

"Are you beginning to see how these individual concepts, when woven into a team, all promote unity and connection? Are you beginning to see that although each element taken alone is strong, when combined, they are stronger than the individual parts?"

"This is really helpful information, Coach Jones. No one has ever talked to the team about any of this stuff. And yes, this is beginning to make sense."

"I'm glad this is proving to be worth your time. I appreciate both of you caring enough about leading your team properly that you are willing to sacrifice your time. This is just a brief introduction to the five leadership traits I want to teach you. Let's move on to the fourth trait."

"Sounds good, coach. What's the fourth trait of the starting five?

"Number four of the Starting Five is mental toughness. In order to be a leader, mental toughness is essential. I know you have all heard the term, and I'm sure everyone has some definition. But if we start out with our same question, perhaps that will guide us better as we examine this great principle."

"I think I know what that question is, coach."

"Go ahead, Dylan, what is it?"

"Does it make the team better?"

"Very good, Dylan, you both are catching on quickly. How much better will we make the team if that question becomes part of our core values? It's exciting to think about how much following that principle can propel us in the right direction.

"I have read stories about Jackie Robinson, a young African American athlete breaking into Major League Baseball. He was sworn at, spit on, humiliated… it was awful. And I'm sure there were many times he knew it was unfair. There were many times he was angry, frustrated and totally ready to quit; but he didn't. He had an exquisite purpose, and his purpose of proving who he could be was greater than the attacks that came at him every time he stepped out in public.

"Mental toughness means there aren't any excuses. It means being so focused on your task that a bad call doesn't matter. A teammate's comment doesn't matter. The coach having an off day doesn't matter. Getting into an argument with a parent or friend on the way to the game doesn't matter, at least, in terms of how you perform. Mental toughness means doing what is most important in the moment without allowing anything else to deter you. To be a captain requires a focus that is trained on doing the right thing. That focus is so steady it encourages your teammate's to be that focused as well."

"Coach, I don't think any player on the team had mental toughness anywhere close to that level last year. Do you think we can accomplish that for this season?"

"I believe we can, Alex. It's a process. We will have to be intentional about learning how to do that. It will mean stopping practice and working through situations where mental toughness wasn't used. There will be many teaching points, but I'm confident we can all learn and grow in this area together. Does that sound good to you?"

"That sounds great to me. I'm really looking forward to all of this."

"Let's talk briefly about the fifth component of the Starting Five. Just as coachability is related to integrity, and work ethic is related to coachability, so is number five interwoven with integrity, coachability, work ethic, and mental toughness. Let me sum up number five with one statement: CAPTAINCY IS A PRESENCE THAT SETS A TONE.

"There is a presence, a body language, a demeanor, that instills belief. There is a presence that makes a team better than the individuals that make up that team. It can take on several different appearances, depending somewhat on personality, but it is the result of integrity, coachability, work ethic, and mental toughness.

"Can I be really honest with you? In all my years of coaching, I have rarely had a player who exhibited all five of these characteristics. Oh, we've had players with two of them, and sometimes three, and there certainly was effective leadership there. However, the really fun and exciting part of having leadership that exhibits all five is the team is better. The teams we have coached with a leader like that won more games than their talent would have predicted.

"Now let me address some issues of leadership that I consider roadblocks. Being a leader always comes under scrutiny, and it is important to function in a leadership role by remembering a couple of things that can undermine your position of leadership. If I could sum up two of these for you to keep in mind, it would be what I could call 'abuse of power' and 'getting to arrogant.'

"If you have navigated the Starting Five well, you don't want to blow it by attitudes that undermine your leadership. Abuse of power and getting too arrogant can certainly do that. You will want your coach to have your back and support your position, but these are two issues that can make it virtually impossible to do so. You want to function in this role in a manner that can be supported by your coach and be respected by your team.

"It can definitely be a balancing act as you want to be a messenger of information that makes the team better without being a gossip. Integrity is a big part of this aspect of being a leader, as there is no place here for randomly joining in when a teammate is having an angry moment or giving away information when the coach is telling you something in confidence.

"Dylan, is this beginning to come together in your mind? Can you see how if our captains have a process to grow in these five areas that it can make the team better?"

"You know, coach, when you started out with this, I was doubtful this could all come together. I really do want our team to be the best it can be this year. I think this is an aspect that I had never considered, but I can really see value in it. Alex and I want to raise the expectations for our teammates this year. We are certainly excited and ready to give it a try. So where do we go from here?"

"Great question, Dylan. We want to go beyond theory and make sure that we adopt these concepts proactively. We don't want to be content just to talk about this, but we want to implement these five as an integral part of our culture. The way I see this playing out is by having conversations between the coaches and the captains. As various issues arise this year, we will search together for solutions and better ways to do things that will make us a better team and help our captains grow as leaders.

"I think we can approach several aspects of our team by considering how many of the starting five attributes could impact any given issue and how we can find solutions. I think as we discuss these issues and arrive at potential solutions we will be better as the season progresses.

"For example, how would you two handle this as captains? We are having a bad week of practice. Your teammates appear tired. Perhaps a few of the players are struggling with bad attitudes. What are some possible ways that the captains and the coach can approach this? Will we approach this from any of the starting five that you feel are appropriate? Alex, any ideas on how we should handle that?"

"Wow, coach, thanks for putting me on the spot. Well, I guess from an integrity standpoint it is important that the captain sets an example of being positive. But to be honest, I think we all get tired sometimes, but I guess my first thought is the integrity of doing my best."

"Very good answer, Alex, and we will develop the concept of integrity a little later. How about you, Dylan? Do you have any thoughts?"

"Yeah, coach, I agree with Alex. I think integrity comes into play here. I mean we need to work hard and do what we say. It also seems like coachability is part of this. I guess work ethic, mental toughness, and a presence that sets a tone also factor into this equation.

It will certainly require mental toughness from the entire team to practice hard on days we may not feel like it. It becomes clear that a captain needs to set the tone even when the captain is tired as well."

"You've made my point here really well. Dylan, I love the five aspects of the Starting Five because they are exactly like the impact of weaving a team together. It becomes better than each individual piece. As you just said, all five of these have a positive impact on each of the other four and because of that, all five have an impact on everything you do as a captain.

"All right then, I think that leads us to discussing each of the starting five in a little more detail. If we increase our understanding of each one, we will increase the impact on making our team better."

Chapter 2 – Ingetrity

"So let's get into a little more depth on integrity. Integrity is the element that binds everything together. I would go so far as to say that in the absence of integrity, it is impossible to be a quality leader. Integrity has to invade every aspect of your life. It has to impact you as you practice, play, lead, and live."

"Coach, it seems to me that work ethic is a bigger deal. I mean, don't you want someone who really works hard to be the captain? I thought to be captain you had to be the hardest working member of the team."

"That's true. A good work ethic is absolutely essential. I would go even further and say that it's not enough to outwork your teammates, but that they actually see you outworking them. It has to happen every day in practice. However, it has to happen in the right order.

"Dylan, we just heard from Alex. What do you think?"

"I kind of agree with Alex. I don't think anyone who lacks a strong work ethic should be a captain. A strong work ethic might be the most important quality a team leader can possess."

"I'm glad you both agree that a strong work ethic is vitally important. As this year's leaders, I'm going to expect each of you to set the tone in practice. I need both of you to be my two hardest workers on the court. I think it will be important for each of you to be the first ones on the floor to start practice and the last to leave. As we discussed earlier, the team needs to see you two outworking everyone else. So, yes, I would agree that having a strong work ethic is incredibly important.

"However, I still believe integrity is the most important and fundamental trait a leader can possess. Alex, you appear like you are processing this. Do you have questions or thoughts about any of this?"

"Well, I'm not sure."

"You are free to ask anything or express any disagreements. I promise I won't make you run too many extra sprints at practice for disagreeing with me."

"Okay, here's what I am thinking. After what you just told us, including your high expectations for us to outwork everyone on the team, it seems like you are placing the highest value on work ethic. Isn't that the case, coach?"

"I know your only experience with me so far is what you saw in our summer workouts and games we played. You will find out quickly that I value and will emphasize the importance of having a strong work ethic. That will be the expectation for every member on the team. In fact, the best chance we have of winning against a team with more talent is to outwork them. Learning how to work hard is something I want you guys to develop, not just for basketball, but it will also help you be successful in life. We will certainly discuss work ethic later, but again, allow me to explain why integrity is the foundation for all other leadership qualities.

"Maybe it would help if you thought of integrity as an umbrella that sits atop the other four and creates a protection. Integrity is an overarching presence that permeates the other four and brings that element of honesty and intention to how you function in each of the other four.

"Both of you mentioned earlier that there are days that you don't feel like working as hard as other days. Is that correct?"

"Coach, we understand the importance of working hard every day because it prepares us for the games. It enhances our ability to cope with unexpected situations that might arise during the course of a game. It helps us learn to stay poised under pressure. I know it's important, but yes, there are days I don't feel like practicing!"

"Why is that Dylan?"

"Coach, I think that answer will likely vary from person-to-person."

"Alex, do you agree with what Dylan just said?"

"Actually, I do coach. Some days are harder than others to show up for practice. Generally speaking, most days I am excited to practice. However, there are other days that I really struggle to be there."

"I appreciate your honesty and transparency. Let's examine why that happens. It's likely, if you two feel that way, I imagine there are days the rest of the team feels that way as well. If the captains demonstrate apathy or a lack of desire about being at practice, those feelings could easily permeate the rest of the team. It might be wise for us to determine the outside factors that contribute to players feeling that way about practice on occasion. Do either of you have any thoughts about this?"

"Some days we are tired from a late night of homework. Some days we may not feel well. Or, perhaps it's late in the season and we are just mentally and physically exhausted. Sometimes it happens after a tough loss the night before, and we haven't quite mentally recovered from the game."

"Those are all understandable reasons. Honestly, there are some days that are a bit more challenging for me as well. I love practice time with my team, but some days are harder than others."

"Seriously, coach! I would have never guessed that. I assumed you would always want to be at practice."

"I do, Dylan. However, just like you guys, some days are more difficult than others."

"Can we ask you the same question, coach? What are some of the reasons that make it harder for you to show up to practice?"

"I'm glad you phrased it that way, Dylan. It's not that I don't want to be at practice, but some days I am also tired. Some days I don't feel well either. Other days certain aspects of life are vying for my attention. So here is the million dollar question. Whether it's the coaches or the players, what do we do on those days we are not physically or mentally positioned to be fully engaged in practice? What do we rely upon to help us practice at a high level when we just don't feel like being there?

"Both of you mentioned that work ethic might be the most important attribute of a captain. What if the captain doesn't feel like working hard that day? Where do you turn when the desire is absent. I mean, if you physically don't want to be at practice, being a great communicator will not help you give 100% effort. Having a great work ethic will not necessarily make you

34

want to give 100% on those days you lack the desire. Being a great encourager won't motivate you to be fully present at practice, and neither will any other traits we might expect from a captain.

"This is why integrity is so instrumental for any leader. Integrity will not allow you to show up and only give 50% effort. Choosing integrity will prevent you from cutting corners when the coach isn't looking. Integrity will not permit you just to go through the motions at practice. It is the driving force that will demand you choose to give maximum effort in the face of adversity.

"Understand there will be days that your 100% effort may look a little different than the previous day, but integrity will hold you accountable to give 100% of what you can give on any given day. One hundred percent is the maximum amount of effort you can give. It sounds good to say you have given 110% effort, but the reality of it is you can only give 100% effort. That's it. You can't give 70% effort on Monday and make up for it by giving

130% on Tuesday. Again, it sounds good to say you are going to give 110% effort, and I certainly understand what is being communicated with that statement; however, it just doesn't work that way. Giving anything less than that is a lost opportunity to make yourself and your teammates better. That is why I believe integrity is the greatest quality any leader can possess. It binds all the other traits together. It is the foundation that gives stability to any leader.

"Executing the other leadership traits well will be a byproduct of leading with integrity. It will increase your influence in every area. When your leadership is elevated to that level, you will have credibility as a leader and your teammates will follow. Can either of you think of any other leadership trait that possesses the power to do all of that?"

"I don't think so, coach. That really makes a lot of sense."

"Well, Alex, let's examine this concept in reverse to illustrate the importance of integrity. I know during the summer workouts you both commented to me that last year's seniors were not very effective in their leadership. Give me some feedback on how you think the team responded to their leadership or the lack of it."

"Coach, it was not good from the start. I think because they were heading into their senior year, they felt they could skip summer workouts. They did not attend weights, plyometrics, conditioning, or the team camp. However, they found time to show up for the summer games."

"Alex, you mean the easy and fun stuff, right?"

"Yes, coach, the easy and fun stuff. They were not committed to the daily workouts, but just wanted to play in the games."

"Dylan, how do you feel the team reacted to their lack of leadership in regard to all of that?"

"It created division from the beginning, coach. The rest of the team didn't feel like they earned the right to be captains. They didn't make sacrifices to be there. They didn't outwork the rest of the team. They didn't encourage anyone, but they certainly criticized us when we made mistakes. They talked behind our backs. They tried to undermine the coaches. We didn't want to lose in the playoffs last year, but I honestly believe the team was happy when the season ended. We were done with that group of seniors."

"Alex, in your opinion, were those seniors vocal leaders?"

"Yes, they talked a lot. Like Dylan said, it was not words of encouragement, but they were at least loud and vocal."

"Dylan, do you think those seniors worked hard?"

"Yes and no."

"What do you mean by that, Dylan?"

"Well, they worked hard in the games, but they demonstrated very little effort in practice or during the off season."

"Do either of you feel they were skilled basketball players?"

"Yes, that was the frustrating part. They were good and we needed them to win games. It was also frustrating because they could have been even better had they paid the price in practice."

"Let me see if I understand both of you. They were vocal leaders? They worked hard during games but not practices? They were skilled athletes who helped the team win some games last year? Is that a fair assessment of last year's captains?"

"That pretty well sums it up, Coach Jones."

"Do you remember earlier in our conversation you both agreed that being vocal, having a good work ethic, and being a skilled player are some of the most important traits a captain can possess?"

"Yes, we remember."

"So, those seniors possessed those traits, and yet, the rest of the team didn't enjoy the season and were eagerly awaiting their graduation. What important trait was missing from the starting five traits of a captain, and don't say a presence that sets a tone. They certainly set a tone, but unfortunately it was a negative one."

"It was integrity, wasn't it coach?"

"You are exactly right, Dylan. That's why I am convinced integrity is the guiding principle. It must be the foundation of your leadership. It truly does bind them all together in a way that creates a cohesive team that trusts and enjoys one another. Without integrity, the other traits will diminish in importance and effectiveness."

"This is starting to make a lot more sense now."

"Coach, even though I wasn't a captain last year, I still wanted to make drastic changes. However, the team was in an awkward position when Coach Phillips became sick and had to retire from coaching with only one month left in the season. I just didn't feel that was the time to create change. Additionally, I didn't even know where to start. If I had known then what I am learning now, it certainly would have helped."

"Well, Dylan, this is the start of a new season. I want to change the culture and want you two to be very instrumental in the process. Building a program and creating culture takes time. However, after seeing you both play and your commitment to the team this summer, I believe we can do this together. If each of you will continue to lead and live with integrity, this upcoming season has tremendous potential. Can I count on both of you to do that?"

"Can we sleep on it and let you know tomorrow, coach? Just kidding, we will do our best. We promise!"

"I'm really glad to hear that. I think this team will experience a great season and have a lot of fun in the process.

"Before we move on to the second trait of the starting five, I want to share a personal story and make a few closing comments. Is that all right with you two?"

"Hey Alex, we better pull up a chair and order some pizza. Coach is reminiscing again and we will likely be here a while."

"Well now, aren't you two quite the comedians. Unfortunately for the team, your comedy routine is more engaging to watch than your jump shots."

"Wow, coach, we didn't know you had it in you. We're just kidding. We really do want to hear the story."

"Let me take a moment to respond to what you just said. I think humor and trust go hand in hand. The fact that we could respond to each other with humor, in safety, indicates a deepening relationship built on trust.

"So, it was my freshman year of college, and we were a couple of weeks into preseason practices. Our coach gave us all a practice routine we followed at the beginning of each practice. He was normally there to monitor our progress and make sure we were executing the skill development aspect properly. However, on this particular day as the team walked onto the court, we noticed coach was not waiting for us.

"By this time we knew what we were supposed to do and we all went straight to work. The team was evenly split on each end of the court. About five minutes into our work out one of the players inquired to the whereabouts of coach. No one knew and so we all went back to our workout. About five minutes later something interesting began to take place."

"What was it, coach? Did you finally make a shot?"

"Nice one, Dylan. I will express my appreciation for your sense of humor during sprints at our first practice next week. Actually, Dylan, this is the portion of my story that I will tie into our discussion on integrity. A few of the players on the other end began to deviate from their workout and started shooting hook shots, half court shots, and attempting to dunk the ball. Within minutes additional players began to join that small group that had broken away from their practice routine. I noticed some of the players on my end of the court began looking around to see if our coach was in the gym. At this point he was still nowhere to be found. To my amazement additional players went to the other end and joined the group that was doing everything except what was expected.

"By this point two-thirds of the team was goofing off while the other third continued their workout. Within moments of that, I was very happy I chose to continue doing my workout."

"Why, what happened next, coach?"

"Alex, our coach was in the sound booth watching everything take place. The lights were off in the booth. We couldn't see him, but he was watching our every move. I guess he was checking to see how his team would respond when he wasn't monitoring the workout. He must have seen enough. His loud voice echoed throughout the gym, and it caught everyone's attention. Those on the other end quickly proceeded to resume their workout, but it was definitely too late."

"What did your coach do or say? I mean how upset was he?"

"Dylan, he walked down the long flight of stairs, and looked at the players on my end of the floor and told us to continue our workout. He then moved quickly to the other end and began having a conversation with the other group. I don't know what was said, but we never had that problem again. Let's just say their conditioning improved dramatically that day."

"I'm guessing you were glad you made the decision to continue your workout? What made you do that coach? I mean most of your team starting having fun. Why didn't you?"

"That's a really good question, Alex. There were a small handful of teammates that continued working out even when we thought coach was not in the gym. I don't completely know why. It's possible there were a few factors that influenced our decision. Perhaps it was fear of getting caught. It's possible we had a deeper commitment to the team. Maybe we just wanted to get better and sticking to the practice routine provided the best pathway. Perhaps all of those were factors, but I would like to think integrity played a part in our decision. It was the right thing to do. That was the expectation our coach had for us, and honoring that was the best decision. Alex and Dylan, integrity matters, and it always will. Making the right choice will consistently reap benefits in the end, and it certainly did for us that day.

"As we evaluate the starting five principles, we must remember to do so in light of our main question:

DOES IT MAKE THE TEAM BETTER? One group of players made the decision to make the team better. The other group made a selfish decision that lacked integrity. Do either of you think their choice to stray from the practice routine made the team better? Do either of you honestly think their choice built trust with the coach?"

"Not at all, coach. If integrity means doing the right thing no matter if anyone is watching or not, then they really dropped the ball."

"I believe both of you are understanding the importance of integrity. Every leader needs to possess and understand the positive impact it can have on a team. To close out my comments on integrity, maybe it would help to have a visual image of integrity:

INTEGRITY is the top of the push-up.

INTEGRITY is the bottom of the squat.

INTEGRITY is running the last sprint as hard as the first.

INTEGRITY is saying I will be there at 5:00, and actually being there at 5:00.

INTEGRITY is saying you will shoot 50 free throws and doing exactly that.

"So, Alex, if you could sum up integrity in a way that makes the team better, what would it be?"

"Hmmm, I guess that your words, your actions, and your attitude all line up in a way that is best for the team. I mean, I've always known about the part with honesty and integrity, but in leadership, it seems like it is a lot more. I hadn't thought about it in terms of hard work or not joining in talking bad about stuff, but I guess it does."

"Good, Alex, can you see how that makes the team better? Can you see how integrity builds connection and unity?"

"Yeah, coach, it's kind of like some of the events from last year when the seniors didn't do stuff like this. We weren't nearly as good as we could have been."

"Great, I think we are establishing some core values that will have a positive impact on our season. Shall we move on to some more depth on coachability?"

"I guess so, coach, but you sure are testing our mental toughness waiting on that pizza to get here."

"Maybe now would be a good time for a short break. There are a few snacks and drinks in my office. Why don't you guys run down and grab those and meet me back here in ten minutes. We will eat lunch around noon. I think those snacks will suffice until then."

Alex and Dylan were glad for a short break as it gave them some time to talk privately. As they were walking to Coach Jones' office they began discussing the information from the meeting.

"Well, Alex, what do you think so far?"

"Honestly, I was interested after what coach explained to us earlier this week, but this has far exceeded my expectations. I am really starting to see tremendous value in this. What are your thoughts so far, Dylan?"

"To be truthful, I was a little reluctant to sacrifice an entire Saturday for this meeting. I thought it would be more leadership information that sounds good in theory, but the kind of information that you have to be in position of power to implement. This isn't like that at all. Alex, we can utilize this information immediately, and this is certainly worth our time. If we will use this to be better team leaders and raise the bar for future captains, I think that would be a great legacy for us to leave the team."

"When you put it in terms like that, it is pretty exciting to think about the impact these principles can have on our leadership. Dylan, you grab the water, and I will carry the snacks. I want to get back and hear what he has to say about coachability."

"Alex, you know me, as long as coach is providing snacks and pizza, I will listen to anything he has to say."

Integrity Discussion Questions:

1.　　Do I keep my word to myself?

2.　　Do I keep my word to my coach?

3.　　Do I keep my word to my teammates?

4.　　Depending on your answers, what is the overall impact upon yourself, your coach, and your teammates?

Chapter 3 – Coachability

"I see you two found the snacks and drinks without any trouble. Let's take a short break from the starting five while we have our snacks. I really think with the group of players I saw this summer at our camps, we have the potential to do really well this season. How do you guys feel about this year's team?"

"We certainly feel the same. Our post players have so much potential to dominate the inside game. We also feel we can utilize our quickness to increase the defensive pressure this year."

"I couldn't agree more, Alex."

"Dylan and I were talking with several teammates last week. Enthusiasm is so much higher than what it was last year. I think this will be a perfect time to implement your new system and certainly the starting five leadership principles."

"Coach, the great news is since we are juniors we will have two years to learn and lead with these principles. The possibility for long term impact is extraordinarily high with time and excitement on our side."

"Dylan, one of the priorities for me as the coach is to teach these principles in such a way that they take root, not just in you two, but in our younger players as well. The ripple effect of this type of leadership is nearly incalculable. I think it's pretty cool you both get the chance to initiate the process. Today starts a journey for each of you that will create a pathway for you to leave a legacy for this program. With that in mind, what do you guys want from me as your coach? How do you see me being the most help to you?"

"Coach, we really appreciate you trusting us to help serve and lead this team, but we also appreciate the time you are taking to invest in us. I guess what we need from you is patience. With what we have heard so far, Dylan and I are completely on board with your plan. I guess we need you to understand this is a new style of leadership for us. We will make mistakes. We will likely forget some of the information from today. Just know those mistakes are not intentional, and we want you to help us work through any issues we might struggle with in the days ahead."

"I can do that, Alex. Just remember we want the same thing and that is to make the team better. Does it make the team better will always be the guiding question that will help determine our best course of action. Well, it looks like you guys are about done with your snacks. Let's take a deeper look into the concept of coachability.

"Alex, if you were asked to define coachability, how would you explain it?"

"Without giving it too much thought, I think the first thing that enters my mind would be doing whatever the coach tells you to do. A coachable player never questions or challenges the coach's authority. A coachable player goes the extra mile. He or she rises above mediocrity and strives to honor the coach by doing more than expected."

"Alex, that's a really good response, especially without having much time to think about it. However, I might push back on one thought you expressed. Before I do that though, I would like to hear from Dylan. What are your thoughts on coachability?"

"Hmmm, I've never really given much thought to it. I think I just assumed the expectation was to do what the coach tells you to do. I mean I've been on teams where certain players tried to undermine what the coach was doing. It was usually because they were upset at the coach about the lack of playing time or something of that nature. I'm pretty sure I simply attributed it to a negative attitude and not so much a lack of coachability. Like I said though, I haven't really thought about it much from that perspective. However, I would agree with Alex's conclusion on the topic."

"I believe you are both right about certain aspects of being a coachable player. However, should a team leader always follow the coach no matter what the instructions are?"

"I think so, coach, but you are making me second guess myself by asking that question."

"As a coach, I certainly desire for my players, and especially my team leaders, to respect my authority and do as I ask. However, I think coachability transcends the basic mindset that the only reason I am doing this is because the coach told me to do it."

"Shouldn't we follow instructions simply because you told us to do something, coach?"

"Alex, I truly believe everything revolves around the relationship. It's incredibly important that trust is built between the coach and the players. When I tell the team to do something, I don't want the team's response to be out of fear. I don't want you guys to blindly do what I ask because you are worried about repercussions. I want the team to jump into action because trust has been established. Integrity and trust are interwoven and the result is a team that listens to their coach. Why? Because they know everything their coach will ask them to do will always be in the best interest of the team. Often times when that trust is missing, many coaches create relational distance to maintain control. Trust will never flourish under this style of leadership. If a coach feels the need to be a dictator to maintain control of his or her team, they are missing the relational aspect of coaching. From my perspective, it would be much simpler to say, do this because I said so. That's the easy path to choose. However, we know deeper relationships enhance and build unity. This unity will foster an environment where coachability is a natural result."

"Coach, I thought being coachable was strictly the player's responsibility."

"Don't misunderstand me, Dylan. So much of coachability falls on the player's shoulders. They have to demonstrate humility. They have to be willing to support the coach. They must listen and respond appropriately to the coach's instruction. However, doing those things doesn't necessarily make one coachable at least not fully."

"Coach, I am a little confused now. How much do you expect from us as leaders in regard to being coachable? Isn't it enough if we are being humble, supporting you as the coach, listening to what you tell us and then doing those things? That seems like a coachable player to me. Am I wrong about that?"

"No, you're not wrong, Alex. It's just an incomplete definition. Being coachable is a deep well of personal sacrifice. Think of it this way. If the player doesn't buy into what is being taught, even if there is a surface level compliance, there isn't a depth that makes them better. In other words, you can go along with what I ask you to do without believing you should be doing those things. How long will that last? How far will that take you? Dylan, I can see the wheels turning. What are you thinking?"

"I assume you mean other than when is the pizza arriving?"

"Yes, something other than when the pizza is arriving would be great."

"Coach, I am thinking what about those situations where maybe we do not agree with you. There may be times that a surface level obedience is all we can give. I mean we either confront you on why we think you are wrong, or we comply on a surface level to give the appearance we are being coachable leaders."

"Dylan, I completely understand and appreciate what you are saying, but do you believe those are the only two legitimate options? I'm confident we can determine a better path than that."

"I agree coach, but what is that better path? I'm sure there will be times in the season that we may not always agree with you. How does a coachable player handle those situations?"

"Dylan, coachability is one of those words that can be difficult to define because it has a tendency to mean different things to different people. We are pretty sure it means listening, doing what we are told, and doing our skills the way the coach says to do them. Even when we define it in those terms, we really don't have that much of a workable definition, do we?

"I think the reason we struggle so much with the concept is because we start with a very backwards way of considering it. Let me explain what I mean. Have you heard the expression, 'When the student is ready, the teacher will appear?' It is backwards from the way we tend to define coachability, but so much more effective. Coachability isn't the coach's responsibility as a motivator; it's yours as someone who wants to play the game well.

"In other words, we need to be ready to be coachable before we can be coachable. Being coachable involves the way you show up before anything else has happened. For me, a couple of words come to mind. One is sponge and the other is heart. When Michael Jordan said he was a sponge, you knew exactly what he meant. It meant he was an ACTIVE listener. He didn't mean he was a hold your eyelids open and try not to look bored listener. It didn't mean he was an already know it all kind of listener. It meant he was paying close attention and anxious to put into practice what he had learned kind of listener. He was a sponge.

"It might help to visualize another aspect of a sponge that we don't give much thought to. A sponge is incapable of soaking up half the moisture. To be a leader you need to be the kind of sponge that not only soaks up all the information, but also serves as a role model for the other members of the team.

"To be a leader, you need to be coachable in a way that serves as an example for your teammates. Captains must ask themselves, does my attitude and coachability make the team better? Coachability must be presented with enough evidence that the entire team believes that you believe. If you want to be honored as a leader, you must honor the leadership above you.

"The second part of this aspect of coachability is heart. We hear the word heart thrown around a lot in sports, but what exactly do we mean? If a sponge is the learning side of the equation, heart is the want to side of the equation. I coached a youth team years ago that only had one tall player, and he was injured in the first game of the tournament. We were playing against kids that were a year older than our team, and frankly, we didn't have a chance in the world to keep a game close, let alone win a game. The kids were pretty discouraged."

"How did you guys handle that, coach?"

"Alex, we called a timeout and discussed the situation with the team, and we came to the same conclusion. We were going back out on the court and play with as much heart as we possibly could. That meant we would dive on the floor after loose balls. That meant we would out work and out hustle the other team. If we were going to lose, our opponents would know they had been in a battle. Playing with heart should never be connected to the score. It should be something you do as part of your character. It's integrity. It's about doing the right thing.

We learned that heart is about what's on the inside, and it shouldn't be affected by external sources.

"Heart as an element of coachability means that once we decide a path as a team, we will pursue it with everything we have. Heart eliminates doubts and questions, and becomes all about effort. It simply isn't enough to nod and act as if we agree when in our heart we know we don't. That hinders effort and outcome, and for the captain the bar is even higher.

"So we combine the sponge with the heart, and we have coachability. In the absence of either one, there is no coachability. And if we can achieve this level of coachability in our captains, they become a carrier. They spread the 'condition' to the entire team. When our captains make the decision that they will actively and visibly be a sponge and play with heart, everyone say it with me, IT MAKES THE TEAM BETTER.

"Dylan, you just asked me how does a coachable player handle a situation when the captain does not agree with the coach. Before I answer that directly, I wanted to share those two aspects of what it means to be coachable. It will help you better understand what being coachable means. All coaches want their players to be active listeners. Every coach also wants their players to demonstrate heart when practicing and playing. If the captain is doing those two things, it will allow more room to approach the coach with questions or concerns. The coaches and captains must develop a relationship that can facilitate respectful exchanges. There is a big difference between questioning the coach and asking questions of the coach. The attitude and motive in which you approach the coach when disagreements arise must be positive, respectful, and sincere. Does any of that make sense to you guys?"

"It makes a lot of sense. It seems the stronger the relationship between the coach and captain, the better the communication will be. That makes perfect sense, but since this is your first year coaching us, we still don't know you that well. Does that impact how we approach you if a situation ever arises?"

"Relational trust is built over time. That trust will come if we continue to focus on what's best for the team. That trust will come even quicker if we operate with integrity. If I can trust the choices you make are in the best interest of the team, I can work with any mistakes you might make. As long as I operate within that same framework, and you trust me to make decisions in the best interest of the team, I think we can manage to work through any problems. Let me close this discussion on coachability with one more thought. I call these the two M's of coachablity.

"**Maturity** is the first one. Being coachable abso-lutely requires a player to be mature. The individual must recognize the need to place the team above themselves. Being a coachable player means receiving constructive feedback in a way that fosters development and personal growth, and that certainly requires maturity. Coachability is the result of a player who chooses to do what makes the team better through the framework the coach has established. It means being open to feedback, because a coachable player recognizes the gap between the current reality of where they are versus where they ultimately want to be. Being coachable will likely mean personal sacrifice at some level. It might necessitate a level of courage to support the coach in the face of opposition from your teammates. Depending on the situation, coachability may very well take on a variety of appearances. Each one requires a level of maturity that is developed over time and through intentionality."

"Coach, what if the player lacks the maturity to be a captain, but they are a great player and they work really hard? Does that disqualify them from being a captain?"

"Dylan, I'm glad you asked that question. Having talent is a good quality for a team leader to possess, but it's not a primary qualification. That may sound counterintuitive to how most teams determine captainship. The problem is, talent alone doesn't solve problems. Talent alone doesn't receive criticism in a way that creates growth. Talent alone is not sufficient. To answer your question directly, leadership does require maturity, and if you lack a certain level of it, that does become a disqualifier. Does that make sense to you, Dylan?"

"Absolutely coach, I have been on previous teams where maturity was certainly lacking from the captains."

"How did that work out for the team?"

"It didn't work out at all. There was constant friction between the captains and coaches and that trickled down to the rest of the team. Having a positive attitude in the midst of a challenging moment certainly requires maturity. Considering everything you have said so far today, I'm pretty sure I haven't really considered what it means to be a captain."

"Unfortunately, I haven't either, coach. It seemed so simple when you said it, but I believe you were right. Most players would articulate that captains simply lead their team on the floor, and they get to meet with the refs for the pregame meeting. It obviously runs so much deeper than that."

"Dylan and Alex, you are beginning to recognize the depth and importance of leadership. It does require personal sacrifice, and every leader needs to be committed to personal growth to maintain a high level of leadership. Are you both still up for this responsibility?"

"I can't speak for Dylan, but I am absolutely up for the challenge."

"Me too, Coach Jones. I absolutely want to be a captain and help lead this team. I also see value in this for all areas of our lives."

"I'm glad to hear that. You both have so much potential to lead this team in a really positive direction.

"Both of you are thinking through this at a much deeper and more meaningful way than most others will. That will help strengthen the influence you have with your teammates.

"Developing your own maturity and coachability will help you have a greater impact on your teammates as well. As your team sees you responding in ways that reflect maturity and coachablity, it should elevate the behavioral expectations for the rest of the team. At that point, it becomes the power of multiplication. The more the team follows your example as you lead with integrity and maturity, it will naturally produce a team of coachable players. Creating, developing, and growing that mindset will enhance your leadership capacity as well as increasing the overall effectiveness of the entire team."

"Coach, Dylan and I have already discussed how we want to change the basketball culture at our school. We want to leave a legacy for those that come behind us. If being coachable players is part of that equation, you can count on us. What is the other 'M' in coachability? You said there were two, and we just covered maturity."

"Alex, I'm glad you both are committed to this. However, changing culture is a process. It will take time and patience. The good news is that if you will apply the starting five concepts in your leadership style, it is entirely possible. Just remember everything falls under the umbrella of integrity. There are no shortcuts. You both must live and lead with integrity as your guiding principle. To answer your question though, mindset is the second 'M' in coachability.

"**<u>Mindset</u>** – Your mindset will influence your outlook on any issue. Once you begin understanding the concept of being a coachable player, your mindset will be a determining factor in adopting and maintaining a spirit of coachability. The concept of having the right mindset is interwoven with having a good attitude. It's having your mind in a position to respond in a characteristic way consistently.

"As your coach, I need the entire team, but especially the captains, to be consistent in how you receive and process my feedback. Your teammates need to see both of you open to learning the game. They need to observe you receiving my coaching and correction with a positive attitude. It goes back to our previous discussion about being a sponge. Are you willing to soak up all the information you can that will help you become better players and leaders? The mindset that you enter practice with each day will directly impact your capacity to receive feedback in constructive and meaningful ways.

Being a coachable player is about adopting and implementing a mindset that allows you to be grateful for the people in your life that want to make you better. This will allow you to change bad habits and be open to new ideas. It's a mindset of growth that will enable you to accomplish more than you could ever achieve on your own."

"Coach, I just read a quote from Pat Summitt. It reminds me of that exact point you just made."

"Dylan, Pat Summitt was a great coach who was full of wisdom. I'm anxious to hear what she said."

"She said, 'Admit to and make yourself accountable for mistakes. How can you improve if you're never wrong?' That seems to go along with what you said about how maturity factors into being coachable."

"You are exactly right, Dylan. Being coachable will require you to take ownership of mistakes. Admitting when we are wrong and taking responsibility for it requires both humility and maturity. That is part of the mindset that coachable players must adopt if they want to grow into the type of leaders that will make a difference on their teams. Coachable players are aware they do not know all. By the way, I would apply that statement to coaches as well. We must constantly be growing and learning so we position ourselves to help grow the athletes we coach.

"Dylan and Alex, why do you think having the right mindset is part of being coachable? I think you both understand the concept of maturity as it relates to being coachable, but I'm interested in hearing your feedback about the importance of approaching this with the right mindset."

"Well, coach, I guess I would equate it to my parents."

"Explain that to me, Alex."

"I guess what I mean is that in the moment I don't always appreciate my parents feedback. Sometimes I personalize their comments too much. Perhaps they are giving me constructive comments about how to study better, how to clean my room better, how to play basketball better because they actually want me to do better. If my mindset is fixed on the fact that my parents truly care about me and sincerely want me to do the best I can, I will receive their feedback in a way that allows me to grow and become better. However, if my mindset is geared toward hearing their comments from the perspective that they are never satisfied with my performance, then I am not likely to apply their feedback in a way that allows me to improve."

"Wow! Alex, that was pretty good."

"I agree with Dylan. That was insightful, Alex. Now apply that to being a coachable athlete and explain that to me."

"Coach, it's obvious you care about us and want to help us become better leaders and better people. Otherwise, you wouldn't be meeting with us on a Saturday. Knowing you care should create a mindset of growth within us as captains. Knowing you want what is best for us should allow Dylan and me to demonstrate a mindset of growth. We should be open to hearing and applying your constructive feedback throughout the season because we know you have our best interest in mind.

"I think it goes back to trust and integrity. If all of us operate with integrity, we can trust one another. That trust will help us maintain the right mindset we need to be coachable players."

"Alex, I have stressed how integrity will influence the other four aspects of the starting five. I'm glad to see you weaving that concept into coachability. You explained that very well, and I believe you have grasped the importance of approaching this with the right mindset.

"Dylan, I also want to hear from you, but I would like for you to respond in reverse. Can you talk about some of the characteristics of a player who is not coachable? "

"Coach, can I approach my answer with observations from previous team leaders I have had?"

"Sure, if that will help you process more easily. And part of integrity comes into play here as well. We can talk about examples, but it's always better not to name names."

"I'm good with that, Coach. I've seen players roll their eyes when the coach tried to instruct them. I've seen players demonstrate disrespect by looking away from the coach when he is trying to teach or correct them. I've observed players talking back to the coach, lying to the coach, demonstrating poor body language, and even talking behind the coach's back to other players. Those types of players make everything about themselves. They are not team oriented. They typically do not celebrate the team's success but only their own. Their mindset is selfish in nature, and I'm guessing that mentality will not create an environment for growth. Is that fair to say, coach?"

"You are spot on, Dylan. As a coach, I can help develop leaders. I can teach you the characteristics of a coachable player, but ultimately, it's up to the players to approach the game and practices with the right mindset that will allow them to receive coaching instructions in a way that fosters growth. I'm not sure a coach can make a player coachable. I can't teach coachability through more drills or repetition. Being coachable isn't some kind of external force that I control for the athlete. It's an internal attitude that requires meticulous attention. In other words, the mindset of being a coachable player demands intentional monitoring every day.

"I want both of you to understand that being coachable accelerates the learning process, and it will create deeper team unity. There is something contagious about the team detecting humility, coachability, and strong levels of integrity from the captains. Does all of this make sense?"

"It does, coach. This session has been very helpful in terms of understanding what is expected from us as the captains. Being coachable is about having integrity, developing our maturity, and certainly bringing the right mindset to practice and games each day. We want to be coachable. We want to set the example in this area for our teammates. As you put it, we want to be sponges. You can count on us, coach."

"I believe that. I am confident both of you will be great captains for our team. Well, Dylan, I have some good news for you."

"What is it, coach?"

"The pizza is here. Let's take a lunch break. We will pick back up with the third element of the starting five after lunch."

Coachability Discussion Questions:

1.   Do I have a relationship with my coach that makes me better?

2.   Do I honor my coach in the presence of my teammates?

3.   Am I open to constructive feedback from my coach?

4.   Do I implement on the basis of feedback?

5.   Does my attitude reflect my coachability?

Ch. 4 – Work Ethic/Skill Development

"Let's get back to work on the starting five concepts. The third area I want to discuss with both of you has to do with work ethic and skill development. While these two are closely connected, they are not necessarily the same thing. However, they are so closely tied together that I didn't want to separate them in terms of their importance. They each belong as a key ingredient that every captain needs to possess. Before we completely move on, I want to tie in integrity and coachability with work ethic /skill development.

"As we already discussed, all five of these concepts are interwoven. It's important for you to understand how they are connected. I fully believe if you see the bigger picture, it will create a deeper level of buy in from both

81

of you as captains. That's very important to me because the more buy in the team sees from the captains, the more likely they will adopt these principles as well.

"Dylan, how do you see integrity being related to work ethic/skill development?"

"I suppose like we mentioned earlier there will be days that we may not feel like working as hard as other days. However, if we practice with integrity we will give maximum effort even on those days."

"That's exactly right, Dylan. You must have integrity with yourself in order to sustain a high work ethic over a long period of time. You must work according to your values and not your mood. Some days you may not want to be at practice, but allowing integrity to govern your values will help you overcome your lack of desire on that particular day. Skill development will never flourish with a diminished work ethic. They are too closely connected.

"Alex, let's hear from you. How do you see coachability tied to work ethic /skill development?"

"Honestly, I'm not totally sure. I'm guessing you will want us to work hard in practice. If we are being coachable, then we will do what you ask us to do. The result of that will be the team working hard and developing our skills."

"All of that is true, Alex. I certainly hope you choose to work hard in practice, and it will definitely speed up the skill development process. Can I challenge you to think about it on a different level though? Your heart needs to be in agreement with the direction and philosophy of the team."

"I agree with that coach, but how does that impact my work ethic?"

"Great question, Alex. Let's say I make a bad end of the game decision and we lose the game. Perhaps you are upset with me as a result and it impacts your attitude the next day at practice. What if you get in an argument with your parents on the way to practice? What if you study diligently for a test and feel totally prepared, but when you get the test back you did much worse than you thought? Do any of those scenarios have the potential to influence your work ethic at practice?"

"Absolutely, coach. Hopefully none of those would impact my work ethic, but I can see how they have the potential."

"What would keep those from impacting how you practice?"

"Well, for starters, having integrity with my team, my coaches, and myself would hopefully help. Working hard regardless of the external circumstances would be the right thing to do, and having integrity would demand I do the right thing in that moment."

"Alex, I really believe you are grasping these concepts. That was a great response, but let me add to that a bit. I mentioned that your heart needs to be in agreement with the direction and philosophy of the team. When your heart is in agreement with the direction the team is headed, those external circumstances shouldn't impact your work ethic. The heart agreement allows you to see the bigger picture. The end result will motivate you to stay true to the process; part of that process is working hard every day in practice. If your heart is not in agreement with the team's direction, there is no chance of maintaining a high work ethic. Being a coachable player will always build trust with any coach. The coach/player relationship will thrive as an environment of trust is established. This environment of trust will open lines of communication that will allow captains and coaches to remedy any problems that might erode your heart being in agreement with the team philosophy. With that in mind, let's talk about how work ethic and skill development are part of the starting five."

"Work ethic in some sense is a relative term because the dynamics of it can change from person to person or team to team. For example, I have coached teams where one or two players would stand apart from the others because of how much harder they worked than everyone else. They became the standard that established the team's work ethic. However, as new players cycled through the program, there were athletes that worked so much harder than players on previous teams. Had all those players been on the same team, there would have been an elevated standard that reshaped the appearance of hard work. It's easy to fall into the trap of feeling like we have a strong work ethic if we compare ourselves to the wrong people. Athletes can become quite comfortable when the standard of hard work is determined by those around them.

"It is imperative that the coach maintains high expectations for the athletes on the team. The coach must challenge the players each day. The coach must push them to work hard, raise the bar of expectations, and not accept mediocrity from anyone. With that said, the athletes must be intrinsically motivated to work as hard as possible. It all comes back to integrity. Players must establish a high standard for themselves and have the integrity to follow through. Deep down inside, every team member knows in their minds whether they are adhering to that standard or not. Integrity will erase hypocrisy. Integrity will not allow you to work hard one day and then lower your personal expectations the next day. It will not allow you to have high standards for your team but not for yourself.

"Alex and Dylan, this is why it's so important for you guys to show up ready to give maximum effort every day. I can establish the routines, drills, and the workouts, but as captains, I need you both to be the presence that sets the tone in terms of how hard the team works every day. Can you both do that for the team?"

"Absolutely coach! We don't want to be negative about last year's captains, but they did not demonstrate a strong work ethic. Their lack of work ethic certainly lowered the expectations for everyone on the team, and we want to be better leaders than that. So, if you feel there are days we are not pushing ourselves as hard as we should, will you let us know?"

"I can certainly do that, Dylan, and I appreciate you guys wanting me to push you and hold you accountable. When the team sees me holding both of you accountable, it provides a better pathway for me to do the same with them as well. Of course, if both of you are out working everyone else, it will also improve your credibility when you, the captains, require more from your teammates.

"Because they are closely connected, our skill development will improve much more rapidly as we increase our work ethic. However, I am also a firm believer in not just working harder, but working smarter. How do you think we can work smarter in a way that leads to better skill development?"

"Coach, one of the things that really bothered me last year was how much wasted time there was at the beginning of practice. Our team would come into practice a few minutes late every day. Players would stand around talking, texting, and shooting half court shots. We would be at least 15 minutes into practice before we really did anything beneficial. That's a lot of wasted time over the span of an entire season."

"Dylan, am I understanding you correctly that working smarter can be defined by using our time wisely, and doing things that will actually enhance our skill development?"

"Yes, coach. That's exactly what I mean."

"I'm glad to hear that because I will certainly have a practice routine in place. When you enter the gym, you will know exactly what is expected. If you two have the self-discipline to initiate the workout as soon as you enter the gym, I believe the rest of the team will follow.

If we are using every minute to develop our skills, we are certainly working harder and smarter.

"Some other areas I feel that will help with skill development by working smarter include repetition so muscle memory is created and maintained. Practicing under duress and learning how to execute effectively while fatigued will better simulate the very game conditions in which we want to excel. Practicing and improving aspects of the game that are related to the position you actually play is working smarter as well. Let's jump into some specific areas and see how this works.

"If I could use one thought to sum up this aspect of The Starting Five, it would be a cycle of activity. It would start with looking at game film and analyzing performance. It would require honesty and objective analysis. It would require humility and a willingness to be coachable at the most extreme end of that concept. It would require a critical analysis with you and the coach that develops a plan to work on those skills in a manner that makes the team better.

"Let's do this with something as simple as setting a screen for a teammate. There are so many things to consider when setting a screen, and yet we tend to ignore the importance of the screen in our concentration on getting our own shot. So many things come into play here. We need to analyze the proper footwork. We need to be aware of our teammate's skill set and what enables our teammate to perform their best at that moment. We need to recognize defensive tendencies of our opponent and what they are capable of in that moment. And even though many of these aspects are out of our control, we need to analyze what role we play and whether or not we are doing it to the very best of our ability.

"So what are some things that should run through your mind in this situation? I need to set this screen in a manner that gets my teammate open. I need to set this screen in a way that gives me the best opportunity to get open as a second option. I need to set this screen in a manner that avoids the foul. I need to have the proper timing. I need to know where my teammates are and where they will be moving to in the play and be ready for what the defense gives me as the play develops.

"So we've looked at the film, we've analyzed it with the coach. What's next? Now we can go to the court and begin to practice what we have analyzed. Start with just the screen itself and do repetitions of just that one element until it can be done without thinking.

The process begins with thinking, but the end is, 'have I practiced this so much I can do it without thinking?'

"Then we can move on to the second aspect of this skill. Perhaps we go to set a screen with a defender in place. Repeat the repetitions again with the coach and analyze the movement. Analyze the footwork.

"The development of any skill is a cycle of events. Analyze. Attempt. Repetition. Analyze. Correct. Repetition. The goal is to be so good at the skill that it can be done without thought. If you have to stop and think about each aspect of what you are doing, you are behind on the play before you start. If you have to think about where your foot is then you are making your brain work on something that diminishes creativity and court awareness and keeps your brain occupied and slow.

"Once you've mastered the pivot with a defender, you are ready to bring in a ball handler and increase the complexity of the task. Now we're working on the footwork of the pivot, but adding the awareness of where our body goes in relation to the defender and the timing in relation to the movement of your teammate. Again, it is analyze, attempt, repetition, analyze, correct, repetition.

"When this has been improved, you can add in receiving the ball back from your teammate after completing the pivot. Catch the ball, turn, read the defense. Have a second defender force you to shoot, dribble penetrate, make the pass, but work on the read.

"This same work ethic and skill development is an integral part of any skill you want to develop in your sport. Ball handling, passing, shooting, all follow a similar pattern.

"Looking at film and being open to constructive teaching followed by the determination to repeat and analyze and repeat and analyze build a skill set as it concurrently builds self-confidence.

"See how the skill development and work ethic go hand in hand? And just as importantly, can you see how your willingness to work at a skill set in a way that motivates your teammates and makes them more open to film and repetition makes you a better captain and in the process makes your team better? I hope you two are getting excited about the potential of what we are talking about here.

"Let's also examine ball handling under the microscope of skill development. It is one of the most pivotal aspects of the game because of the many other areas of the game it impacts. Alex, you are going to be the point guard this year. What are some things we can do that will allow you to develop your skill in this area of the game?"

"I should consider increasing the amount of time I spend working on dribbling drills each day. I should figure out how to better simulate game conditions when practicing. I could watch more elite ball handlers and mirror some of the things they do."

"I believe all of those things would be helpful, Alex. However, let's break this down a bit more. I will see if I can get our video team to put together some game footage from last year that allows us to evaluate situations where you lost the ball as well as completed a great move. We can sit down together and analyze specifically what led to the turnovers. Did you make the wrong move at the wrong time? Did you use improper technique? Did you try and perform a move you had not mastered yet? Was the ball not positioned correctly in relation to your body to provide the best protection? Was your footwork done properly to most effectively use the ball screen?

"Breaking it down at this level will take time. However, if you are serious about skill development and being the best you can be, this degree of commitment is required. Do you now see the connection between work ethic and skill development? You have to be willing to pay the price to shrink the gap between where you are and where you want to be. Many athletes are not willing to make that sacrifice. This level of commitment will separate you from most other athletes. If you and Dylan will work at this level, your teammates will be put in a position of whether to follow your example or not. The stronger the two of you are in this commitment the more likely your teammates are to follow.

"If we can paint a clear vision of where we are headed and how we get there, I believe we can bring the team with us. Can you imagine the return on that investment? If we can get buy in from the rest of the team to consider this approach to skill development, we can have a really special season."

"Coach, I love the idea of the entire team breaking down game and practice film. If we are analyzing the areas we need to improve with the coaches, and then practicing that specific aspect over and over until we master it, the entire team's skill development will increase tremendously."

"That's exactly right, Alex. If the team remains coachable, and allows the staff to determine specific areas for individual skill improvement, we will be well on our way."

"With all due respect coach, Alex and I don't want to be well on our way. We want to help the team actually achieve our goals and arrive at the destination. How do we make that happen?"

"Dylan, that is a great question. So far we have discussed integrity, coachability, and work ethic/skill development. The last two concepts of the starting five are mental toughness and a presence that sets a tone.

Don't forget all five of these build on one another. To skip one of these steps will diminish the other four. Most importantly, we must never forget that integrity binds them all together. It is the foundation in which the other four are built. There has to be a consistency of character.

"If you two really want to help the team achieve our goals, you must focus on the process and not the end result. The end result is the big picture, and we must not lose sight of that. However, our focus must always be in the moment. Today's practice must demand our attention. The specific drill we are doing in that moment needs 100% of our concentration. We can be motivated by a state championship, but we have to practice in the moment, and we have to do that every day. Again, it's in those moments of the daily grind that you get to be leaders. Having mental toughness and being a presence that sets a tone will be two important determining factors. Are both of you ready to move on to the last two concepts of the starting five?"

"Yes, we are coach. However, this is a lot to digest and a little intimidating to think about implementing."

"It sure is, Alex, but it's all part of the process. Establishing, developing, and maintaining these leadership qualities doesn't end with this meeting today. I will help you develop them over the next two seasons. There will be many teaching points along the way that will allow us to work through each of the five traits. It will all come together. Let's move on to mental toughness."

Work Ethic/Skill Development Discussion Questions:

1.   Does my work ethic elevate the team's effort?

2.   How would I evaluate my work ethic on a 1-5 scale with 1 being poor and 5 being a very strong work ethic? What steps do I need to take to grow closer to the five rating?

3.   What are three areas I need to work on to make the team better?

Chapter 5 – Mental Toughness

"Coach, before you start by asking us what we think mental toughness is, I've always been a little confused by this term."

"Why is that, Dylan?"

"To be completely transparent coach, I'm not totally sure. I guess I've heard coaches and other people mention it, but they never gave an explanation for it. It's not sufficient to tell someone to be mentally tough without determining the expectations that go along with it."

"That is so true, Dylan. Many people emphasize the importance of being mentally tough, but I'm not sure that is very helpful to most athletes if the term is isolated from a clear explanation. With that said, it is a required trait for athletes to possess, and especially athletes that want to lead their teams.

"Basketball is a long season with many obstacles along the way. When you think about the duration of the season, fatigue, injuries, sickness, losing close games, poor performances, the stress of school, homework, relationships, and all the other issues athletes must deal with, it gives you insight into the importance of being mentally tough."

"Coach, we agree that mental toughness is really important. Thinking back to last season is reason enough to convince us of its importance, but how do we develop that trait as leaders?"

"Alex, none of this happens overnight. All of this really is a process, but there are certainly things you can do now to become mentally tougher. Let's jump into this and see if I can bring some clarification.

"We tend to think that mental toughness is some mystical presence that makes us good when we need to be good. We can scrunch our eyes and wiggle our nose and winning behavior shows up.

"The reason I like The Starting Five as a concept for leadership is the way all five elements are interwoven. The previous elements are all necessary as building blocks for mental toughness.

For example, integrity is foundational to the development of mental toughness. If you say what you mean and do what you say, then your teammates can count on you in tough moments and know what to expect. But do you know what is even more important than your teammate's counting on you in tough moments?.......YOU COUNTING ON YOU IN TOUGH MOMENTS. Mental toughness is grown as you consistently keep your word to yourself. If you know in your heart that you have kept your word to yourself and practiced hard and smart, then you have more confidence in yourself and your ability to play with what the game presents you in the moment.

"Integrity means you have worked on basic things in a way that makes you better and makes you more ready to perform at key moments. A lack of integrity with yourself has the exact opposite effect, and it is twofold. Number one, you are not prepared to carry out the play that is important in that moment, and, just as importantly, your own mind doubts because your mind knows you have lied to yourself. Unfortunately, both of these factors double down on derailing mental toughness development.

"As we have previously discussed, integrity is a key element in coachability, but coachability is also a key element in mental toughness. As coachability is about your heart in playing together as a team, it also creates trust in the system that the Coach has implemented for the team. I would venture to say that lacking coachability makes it virtually impossible to be mentally tough and stay in the moment.

"It is when you have trust in the system that you have confidence in your actions in the moment. Key moments that are approached with confidence build mental toughness. Can you see how you cannot single out any of the five traits and expect to have any of them fully develop individually?"

"I do now, Coach Jones. When you first commented about how they are so closely connected, I wasn't sure I understood or agreed. However, as we move along with each trait, it is really making much more sense now."

"I'm glad to hear that, Alex. It's important for each of you to understand how these are connected."

"Me too, coach. Also, I'm better understanding the concept of integrity binding them all together. "

"Dylan, integrity truly is the foundation for all of this. If you two understand the importance of integrity and choose to lead with it, the rest of this will fall in place. Let's continue.

"One of the key elements of coachability is a willingness to prepare, and a key part of preparation and work ethic is fitness. It would be ridiculous to try to be mentally tough without fitness. In the fourth quarter, if you aren't fit enough to make plays, don't expect mental toughness to help you overcome lack of preparation.

"There is an interesting added bonus to fitness in that by the mere desire and effort to improve your fitness beyond that of your opponent, you are developing mental toughness. The willingness to 'go beyond' in fitness in itself grows mental toughness. There is a level of mental toughness in being confident that you have prepared your body for just this moment.

"So we can see that integrity, coachability and fitness/preparation play a role in mental toughness. Let's look at a few things that can very effectively hinder and or stop mental toughness. The first thing that comes to mind is anger. I have seen very few athletes that have been able to improve their performance with anger. I have read that Roger Federer, the all time great tennis player, has discussed having an anger problem early in his career. He came to the realization that his anger issues would keep him from being the player he wanted to be. It is life changing to recognize that anger is truly destructive in your life and make a conscious decision to change.

"Have you ever stopped to think about some of the issues that create anger in your performance? My dad was a coach, and he tended to coach with some anger. He was my hero, and I wanted to be like him. As a consequence, I grew up playing with some anger. But as with most things in life, the real responsibility for anger issues falls on us. And many of the things we have just talked about are the culprit of this self-limiting scenario. If mental toughness is grown as you consistently keep your word to yourself, anger is just the opposite. What tends to create anger? For many of us, it is the duplicity of what we think we can do versus what we have prepared to do. And nothing makes this more of an issue than a 'big moment.'

"Having integrity to ourselves has the effect of shrinking this gap. As we keep our word to ourselves, as we practice with intention, as we develop our fitness, as we as a team are coachable, we are constantly shrinking the gap. As we don't maintain our integrity to self, as we shortcut practice, as we cheat our fitness, as we undermine coachability, we make the gap bigger. This is why we can't magically create mental toughness as some separate skill. It is far to intertwined with the other skills.

"We can certainly enhance our mental toughness by being 'in the moment,' but I for one have struggled to understand the concept, let alone implement it in my performance. For me, that is compounded by the confusion that if I am thinking about being in the moment I am probably already out of the moment. Dylan, any thoughts on some things that might take us out of the moment?"

"Well coach, I suppose things like poor officiating, a missed shot, being distracted by something that happened before the game, and many other things as well."

"Dylan, all of those have the potential to prevent us from being in the moment or take us out of the moment. And then as coaches, we yell your name and tap on our temple, and that might be more distraction than help.

"As with all the other elements in The Starting Five, I think the mental toughness of being in the moment starts with the same basics and builds on them. Integrity builds coachability, which builds work ethic, which builds repeatability, which builds muscle memory, which grows the ability to perform in the moment without conscious thought which is 'in the moment.' Mental toughness has its foundation in very basic repeatable acts, which when repeated well with intention build on themselves.

"There is a certain attraction to addressing mental toughness in this manner. We have always approached mental toughness from the wiggle your nose, scrunch your eyes mystical perspective. And because of that, truthfully, not much of it shows up. People who have it get better and people who don't have it get worse. But by approaching it in this manner, as another element in skill development, it gives us a way to develop a process.

"As with any process, the development of mental toughness must start with recognition. Just as we must recognize we need to be more fit, or get better at free throws, it doesn't take much introspection to reach the conclusion that we are indeed weak in the area of mental toughness. What are the areas of your game that are causing the most distraction or lack of performance? What are key moments in the game when I wanted to do better but didn't?

If we then define mental toughness as being able to do our best in the moments we need to do our best, we can begin to recognize the areas where we need improvement. Think about some sentences that might give you a clue.

I got really frustrated when, is a great place to start. For example,

I got really frustrated when I shot 12% from the field.

I got really frustrated when I let my man score the winning basket.

I got really frustrated when I missed my free throws.

I was mad because I didn't get to play much.

It wasn't fair that.......

"You get the point. Many things can be really upsetting and distracting and the first step is recognizing what these things are. Do either of you have an idea why recognition is so important as a first step?"

"I think so coach, but it seems too simple."

"No need to over complicate the process, Alex. What are you thinking?"

"Well, once we recognize the issue, we can then make a decision about whether we want to address it or not."

"That's exactly right, Alex. Once we have recognition, we are ready to do something about it. The key thought in my mind for this is Stephen Covey. He calls it his 'Circle of Influence.' Covey says it is important to recognize the things in life that you can do something about and the things you cannot. The development and growth of mental toughness is all about The 'Circle of Influence.'

"We then begin to place the elements we can do something about inside The circle of influence. I can do something about my free throw percentage. I can do something about my defensive foot work. I can do something about my field goal percentage. On the other hand, the referees, the coach's decisions, and personal issues off the court, are not inside the circle and are not only a waste of time and energy, but can so escalate the frustration level that makes mental toughness a virtual impossibility."

"Coach, that makes perfect sense in relation to what happen with last year's team. Alex and I spent too much energy trying to deal with things out of our control; or as you put it, outside the circle. You are correct in the fact that it depleted our energy and wasted our time."

"I'm glad you can see the practical benefit of this, and that's why it is important in this process to recognize what is really causing you issues in this regard. Let me give you an example. Have you ever gotten so mad at the ref when you were up 40 that you just couldn't play well? If so, it might be an indication that we can tend to direct our anger and frustration at an easily available excuse rather than the true villain and something that is within our circle of influence.

"Begin to chronicle and recognize the areas of your game that frustrate you and in each of those areas, with the help of your coaches, devise a plan to get better at that. For example, let's use free throws. It always seems funny to me to watch a player miss two free throws and then go through all the body language of unbelief and anger as if there were some mystical force in the universe that blocked the shots. Now we have two problems, the missed points and the potential body language effect on that person and his teammates.

"Is the referee's call inside your circle? Probably not. Is getting better at free throws inside your circle? When you look at it like this, it becomes easier to recognize, doesn't it? The next step, then is developing an effective, smart method for developing this skill. I want to have repetition, but I want the repetition to be in a manner that I can chart and see how I am doing.

But part of the problem might be nerves, so I want to practice free throws in a way that, as closely as possible, duplicates game conditions. However, fatigue at the end of the game can be an issue, so I want to prepare in a way that helps me get better at that aspect of free throws. But my form might be off so I might need some coaching help with my form.

"Mental toughness takes a lot of separate elements in its development, doesn't it? It takes recognition. It takes introspection. It takes a willingness to separate the things we can do something about from the things we cannot. It takes an integrity to self to practice smart and be coachable. It takes repetition and muscle memory. It takes time. And, like all the previous elements of The Starting Five, it cannot be separated from integrity, coachability, or skill development.

"Here are some things to consider when working on your mental toughness. There is always talk about mental toughness, but it seems there is rarely information that increases mental toughness. Let's try to address mental toughness in a way that gives us a pathway to developing mental toughness.

"First, it is important in practice, to be willing to fail or look bad. It is impossible to grow your mental toughness if you aren't willing to expand the area where stress occurs and make it much larger. In practice, push yourself to the point of failure. Failure is the point at which mental toughness begins. Have either of you had anyone tell you to push yourself to the point of failure?"

"I haven't."

"What about you, Dylan? Have you been told that in the past?"

"I don't think so. I mean I've had coaches and even my parents tell me to push myself as hard as I can, but never in the context of developing mental toughness. That does make perfect sense though. If we are never pushed out of the framework of our comfort zone, then even if we possessed mental toughness, there would be no need for it. Coach, what are some other examples of how mental toughness is developed through this process?"

"Dylan, another example would be understanding that self-evaluation also begins at the point of failure. In practice, WANT the ball more. Invite more defense. Push yourself beyond your comfort zone. Increase your presence as a teammate. Recognize your court position in relation to your teammates and the ball. Does your court position and body language send a message of being totally present and wanting the ball when the pressure is on?

When pressure is turned up, the tendency is to turn from it and avoid it. However, the response that builds mental toughness is the opposite. The response that builds mental toughness is going toward the pressure and being willing to accept the consequences. Invite the pressure, respond to it, and then self-evaluate. Did I move into the pressure? Did I get out of my comfort zone? Did my body language send a positive message to my teammates? Did I have positive self-talk? How could I be better in this situation? Is my fitness level high enough to allow me to attempt this? Has my coachability enabled me to learn the skills that I need in this situation? Has my preparation put me in a place to perform in this tense situation?

"Let's take a game situation and see if we can develop a plan for increasing mental toughness. If mental toughness is a skill, then we should be able to practice it and enhance it in a practical, developmental way.

"Let's take a situation where your point guard has the ball and is heavily defended and you are playing off the ball. Maybe in the past this is a time when you have tried your best to look like you don't want the ball. How can we increase mental toughness in this situation? Preparation would come into play, as it is important to know angles and where to go to receive the ball. It is also critical for proper footwork to avoid the travel. If it's towards the end of the game and a close game, then you would know you are going to be swarmed with defensive pressure and possibly fouled. It then becomes important to be able to maintain possession of the ball with at least two people determined to take it away from you. Body language comes into play as it is important to send the message that you've got this.

"The development of mental toughness does not just show up by accident in this situation. Hoping does not make it so. The question then becomes what's my next step? An answer that gives you a pathway is, can I break this situation down into segments that allow me to institute the process: evaluation, design a practice situation, practice, evaluate, practice.

"In this scenario, it would be helpful to evaluate how you respond to a double team. If that response is, I lose my poise or I panic then it gives us an idea of what needs work. That means we can start with getting better at being double teamed. We then start with the ball and two teammates double teaming us. We can practice maintaining ball control and proper footwork while keeping poise under pressure. Everything comes into play here. Have we had the integrity to work on our footwork? Do we have proper technique because we are coachable? Are we fit and strong and able to hold off the strength of the defenders?

"Work on maintaining ball control, poise and footwork. Then stop and evaluate. Get input from your coach and teammates. Stop to evaluate and think through the process before repeating the drill. Then repeat the drill with the double team, maintain poise, proper footwork, and strength. Repeat the drill with self-evaluation several times until you can mentally feel better about how you are handling the situation.

"You are then ready to implement the drill into a similar situation with your point guard starting with the ball. Make yourself available. Practice good body language with good facial expression and work at convincing your teammate that you indeed do want the ball. Then repeat the ball control, footwork, poise under pressure and then self-evaluate. You should feel your confidence growing and, concurrently, your mental toughness. And it's ok at that stage to celebrate your accomplishments. Then you are ready to put this part of your game into the scrimmage part of your practice.

"Can you see how being intentional with your process and practicing each component can develop mental toughness? But it comes because you have been faithful and intentional in the development with integrity of coachability, fitness, skill development, and work ethic through a definite plan. Mental toughness is grown in practice as you move toward the stress. When you add in positive self-talk, repeatability and self-evaluation, it enables you to be intentional about developing mental toughness.

"This process can be applied to any part of your game. Evaluate where you struggle. Break it down. Practice intentionally with integrity. Self-evaluate. Repeat the drill. Self-evaluate. Maintain poise. Move toward the stress. Expand the scope of the drill.

"Mental toughness is essential to success, but it doesn't show up by accident. Like any other skill, it takes work and attention to detail, but it pays off. One of the greatest feelings in sport is meeting the challenge of the moment and performing at the level you want to perform at because you are prepared. Does all of that make sense?"

"It does coach, and it really is exciting to think about preparing for this season in a way that will allow us to play at our highest level. If we struggle in a game the night before, we will understand how to be mentally tough enough not to allow that to diminish our work ethic in practice the next day. These concepts really are interwoven. What did you say was the last characteristic of the Starting Five?"

"The last characteristic of the Starting Five is a presence that sets a tone. I think we are ready to move on to that. Why don't you guys take a five minute break and we will meet back here in a few minutes?"

"Sounds good, coach, and thanks again for taking time to invest in us like this. See you in a few minutes."

Mental Toughness Questions:

1.   Do I focus on the main thing instead of distractions?

2.   Do I stay balanced? Am I too high or too low when performing?

3.   As a leader, does my mental toughness inspire mental toughness in my teammates?

4.   Am I mentally tough enough to respond to adversity in a way that makes the team and myself better?

Chapter 6 – A Presence That Sets a Tone

"A presence that sets a tone is actually my favorite of The Starting Five. But it is also the hardest to verbalize. I mean, yes, it does combine all the other four elements. And yes, it is a process that comes together with work and a process that journeys through integrity, coachability, work ethic, and mental toughness, but it is so much more than that. So let me tell you a story that I think epitomizes the concept far better than my feeble attempt to describe it.

"On a soccer field long ago there was a young college sophomore who exhibited many of these qualities, and he loved playing soccer. But before he could really get the season off to a kicking start, he ran into the goalie's knee with his knee and, sadly, he fractured his kneecap and was out for the season."

"Coach, I can't imagine how hard it would be to miss any part of the season, but the entire season, that would be terrible."

"Yes, Alex, it is terribly difficult to miss an entire season. Unfortunately, in this case it gets worse. On their first away game of his junior season, the team was in a one van accident that resulted in the vehicle sliding upside down and backwards down the interstate. Unbelievably, there was only one injury. Our young soccer player gets glass in his previously injured knee, and, yes, you guessed it, he was again out for the season.

"At this point in our story, our young hero questions what to do for his senior year. Should he go out for his senior year, or should he not? We all face decisions like this don't we? We have to decide something and we simply don't have all the information. There's a new coach. You've missed two years. You're a senior.

"What do you do at this point? And of course, if you have followed the previous four elements, maybe they will help you with this decision. What would integrity tell you to do? How can you be coachable in this situation? Does work ethic come into play here? What about mental toughness? Hopefully at this point, at the very least, your answer is maybe. But an interesting turn of events developed that summer."

"What happened that summer, coach? Did it cause him to play or not?"

"Well, he attended a university that does summer mission trips, and he had participated in these opportunities both of his previous summers. This summer he had the opportunity to go to South Africa. But more importantly, that summer he would take several members of the soccer team with him. He would be the team leader. He would schedule soccer games against schools and prison teams. He would model giving, heart, and core values. And yes, he would make the decision to play soccer that senior season. He would be on the team whether he started or not.

"But he didn't start. As a matter of fact, he wasn't playing all that much. But a funny thing happened. When it came time to elect captains, apparently the team recognized that element of integrity, the work ethic, the mental toughness. They recognized heart. They recognized a presence that sets a tone. A true presence sets a tone that is recognized. It inspires. It makes the entire team better. It is contagious. It wins close games. It causes teammates to play harder. They compete harder. They practice harder."

"So what happened that season?"

"Well Alex, as the season wore on, he played a little more and then a little more. And the fun result of it was that when he was on the field they played better than when he wasn't. And for the first time in school history, his team qualified as one of the four teams to compete for the conference championship. Two games against the top seeded teams were the reward for a great season.

"In the first game, against the second seeded team, our young leader didn't start and his team immediately went down 1-0. He subbed in at right mid and you could sense the difference. They were immediately a better team. He got an assist and they tied the game, and they went on to win that game and get a spot in the championship game against the one seed.

"In the finals, he didn't start again, and eight seconds in, they were down 1-0. Eight seconds. And I know, I know, you can see where we are going here. He came in, got an assist and tied the score, and it remained that way till late in the game, when a key defender was red carded and they were a man down against the 1 seed, tied, and late in the game. It's a great set up for a presence that sets a tone, isn't it?

"Integrity, coachability, mental toughness, work ethic, poise, heart.....it's all part of the equation. But let's throw in another curve. Let's throw in moving our hero out of position to defender. Let's suddenly, in the heat of the most important game of the season move him to defender. Let's move him to a position he simply never plays, and let's do all that at the end of the game against the best team in the conference."

"So, what happened next? Did his team win?"

"Well, at the end of regulation, the game was still tied, and no, he didn't score the winning goal. He didn't,.... but his teammate did. They won the game. They won the conference championship. They won their way into the post season. He was even selected to the all- tournament team.

"A presence that sets a tone isn't some mystical undefinable unobtainable dream. It's hard work. It's heart. It's confidence. It's repetition in practice when you're too tired to do repetition. It's doing what you say you'll do. It's honoring your coach and your teammate's. It's doing all the things that you do in a way that makes your entire team better.

"A presence that sets a tone absolutely has to start with integrity. It has to start with honor and having the back of your teammates and coaches. You have to do what you say. Your speech and actions have to be in sync. And this has to be so true that your teammates have absolutely no doubt that you are who you say you are.

"A presence that sets a tone requires coachability at the highest of levels. Your teammates must totally believe that you respect the coach and the coach respects you. You should feel free to question the coach when it is the two of you, and the better your relationship, the better the positive impact on the team.

"A presence that sets a tone requires a work ethic and skill development that sets a model for the work ethic and skill development of the entire team. It might be important to you to work on skills in another venue and that may help you a lot, but your teammates need to witness you as the leader working on these skills in their presence.

"A presence that sets a tone requires mental toughness that inspires your teammates in the midst of high stress moments. Your teammates need to see a 'we've got this' body language and facial demeanor. A team leader does not get to show doubt. A presence that sets a tone MAKES THE TEAM BETTER."

A Presence That Sets a Tone Discussion Questions:

1.   Is my team better because I am there? If so, describe how the team is better. If not, evaluate areas you might consider changing.

2.   Does my presence enhance integrity and coachability?

3.   Are we better in big moments because of my presence?

"I think I am speaking for Dylan as well, but we both have learned so much today. We understand mastering these traits will take time because it is a process of growth. We certainly want to be a presence that sets a tone for our team this season."

"I know you both want that very much. I'm confident you both will be great captains. Let me put some closure on this, and then I will let you guys go so you can enjoy the rest of your day.

"The Starting Five, integrity, coachability, work ethic, mental toughness, and a presence that sets a tone, have one common thread running through all of them. That common thread is honest self-examination. The only way to grow as a leader is by constantly and honestly examining yourself and realizing where you started and how far you've come and, of course, how much further you have to go. The Starting Five is a never ending journey of introspection. It is coming to grips with your own heart. It is understanding your motives and what drives you to be a better leader.

"Leadership is driven by an honest evaluation of your heart. What do you expect to get out of this? Why are you willing to step up and be responsible? As every event unfolds, can you continue to function well as the captain even when there will be times of disappointment and unmet expectations? There will be times that you will be misunderstood and maligned. There will be times that you will be the topic of unfriendly conversations. Can you continue to be a leader when your friends question what you are doing? In addition to honest self-examination, the Starting Five requires that you have a willing-ness to make yourself vulnerable to the correction and scrutiny of your coach/mentor. When you are willing to face truth without hurt feelings or resistance, it not only enhances your path to improvement, but it makes the entire team better. One of the most difficult aspects of leadership to grasp is the concept of honoring the authority over you in order to instill that same attitude in your teammates toward their captains.

"Being a captain is an honor. If selected properly, it is a statement of faith from your coach and teammates. It is a responsibility that must be taken seriously. Being a captain is so much more than leading your team on the court and meeting with the refs before the game. I think you both understand that after today. I'm looking forward to coaching and mentoring both of you this season. We must remember that integrity and trust will enhance our relationship and will allow for better and more meaningful conversation to take place this year.

"I want you to feel free to ask for help, advice, or clarification any time you need it. This should be a great season for us, and it all starts next week. Let me leave you with two last reminders. Integrity binds all elements of the Starting Five together. Choose to live and lead with integrity. Lastly, don't forget our foundational question we should always ask ourselves."

"We got this coach. DOES IT MAKE THE TEAM BETTER?"

Reference Page

Chapter 1

P.7

1.   Brene Brown, Daring Greatly (Penguin Group, 2012), p. 11

P. 10

2.   www.azquotes.com/quote/882072 - Michael Jordan

Chapter 3

P. 46

1.   https://247sports.com/Coach/3630/Quotes/Admit-to-and-make-yourself-accountable-for-mistakes-How-can-you--35997126/#quote – Pat Summitt

Chapter 5

P. 68

1.   "From Mr. Angry to Mr. Perfect," www.thelocal.ch/20170715/roger-federer-from-mr-angry-to-mr-perfect

P. 71

2.   Stephen Covey, The 7 Habits of Highly Effective People (Simon and Schuster, 1989), 82-88